Crating & Kenneling

FOR

DUMMIES®

MINI EDITION

by Susan McCullough,
Tracy Barr, Sarah Hodgson,
Jack and Wendy Volhard, and
Gina Spadafori

WILEY

Wiley Publishing, Inc.

Crating & Kenneling For Dummies®, Mini Edition
Published by
Wiley Publishing, Inc.
111 River Street
Hoboken, NJ 07030-5774
www.wiley.com

Copyright © 2011 by Wiley Publishing, Inc., Indianapolis, Indiana
Published by Wiley Publishing, Inc., Indianapolis, Indiana
Published simultaneously in Canada

For general information on our other products and services, please contact our
Customer Care Department within the U.S. at 877-762-2974, outside the U.S. at
317-572-3993, or fax 317-572-4002.
For technical support, please visit www.wiley.com/techsupport.
Wiley also publishes its books in a variety of electronic formats. Some content that
appears in print may not be available in electronic books.

ISBN: 978-1-118-01354-0
Manufactured in the United States of America.

10 9 8 7 6 5 4 3 2 1

WILEY

Table of Contents

Introduction

● ●

*I*f your love for dogs began when you started watching TV shows such as *Lassie* when you were a kid, the idea of putting your dog in a crate probably takes a little getting used to. The image of Timmy and his glorious Collie wandering over rolling hills of farmland just doesn't square with the idea of confining your Fido in a plastic or wire enclosure. "Dogs don't belong in cages," you may protest. "It's cruel." But if Fido could speak for himself, he'd probably disagree with you.

For people who love dogs, the crate can be a dandy training tool. Using a crate for house-training, for example, just prompts a dog to do what comes naturally — that is, avoid soiling her den. Her inborn desire to refrain from eliminating in her den teaches her to hold her pee or poop until she can leave, helps her develop bowel and bladder control, and gives you the opportunity to show her where she's supposed to go. But you don't have to confine your use of the crate solely to house-training. You can also use it to keep your dog out of trouble when you can't watch her and keep her safe when she's traveling.

About This Book

Crate-training your dog gives you peace of mind, it gives your dog his own den, and it helps you perform one of the most important training tasks any dog owner faces: house-training. Of course, crates are useful for several other things, too. So that you can find all the information you need to get the most out of crate-training, this book tells you only what you need to know and makes that information easy to find.

In this book, you'll find information like

- ✔ What kinds of crates are good for what kinds of functions
- ✔ Where to set up your crate and what to put in it
- ✔ How crating your dog helps with house-training

This mini book is designed so that you can jump into and out of it at will, reading just what you want to get the information you need. Use the table of contents or glance through the headings to find the information you want.

Conventions Used in This Book

A book as straightforward as this doesn't need complicated conventions, and these are pretty simply:

- ✔ *Italic* is used for emphasis and to highlight new words or terms that are defined.
- ✔ **Boldfaced** text is used to indicate the action part of numbered steps.

We try to alternate between male and female pronouns when referring to pets and humans, but we can't promise it's exactly 50/50.

Foolish Assumptions

In writing this handy guide, we made certain assumptions about you:

✔ You have a dog or plan to get one and you've heard that crate-training is the way to go.

✔ You want to find a safe, humane way to confine your dog when you're not around to watch him.

✔ You've heard that crate-training makes house-training easier and you want to find out how it works.

Icons Used in This Book

Each of the icons used in this book indicates a different kind of information:

 This icon highlights easy alternatives, short-cuts, or other bits of advice that make the task at hand a little easier.

 This icon marks important concepts that can help you in the future.

 If something can go wrong or make a given task harder, you'll see this icon.

Where to Go from Here

This book is organized so that you can go wherever you want to find the information you need. Want to know how to determine the proper size of a crate for your growing puppy? Head to Chapter 2. If you're interested in how to help your dog to like his crate, go to Chapter 3. By using the table of contents or simply flipping through the book, you can find whatever information you need. If you don't know where to go, start in Chapter 1, which explains the basic premise and process for crate-training your dog. If you want even more advice on crating and kenneling, check out the full-size version of *Housetraining For Dummies* — simply head to your local book seller or go to www.dummies.com!

Chapter 1

Crating and Kenneling Basics

. . . .

In This Chapter

▶ Stocking up on crate-training supplies

▶ Identifying the advantages of crate-training — for both you and your dog

▶ Understanding the positive training method

. . . .

*F*ew objects are more important to a wild or domestic canine than the den — that safe, secure place that the animal can call his own. A crate makes a perfect doggie den, re-creating that feeling of security and protection for your dog. Because a crate is open on one side but enclosed on the other three, it offers the dog a safe, secure window through which he can watch his world.

Dogs who are introduced to the crate at a young age soon grow to love their special spaces, and an older dog can learn to at least tolerate a crate when introduced to one properly. Either way, the attachment is well worth cultivating because a dog crate functions as a bed, a car seat, a house-training center, and a puppy haven all in one. And dogs can *love* them.

This chapter introduces you to crates and crate-training, and because how you go about training your dog can help or hinder your efforts, it also explains the principles behind the dog-training method used in this book.

What You Need to Crate-Train

Although dogs like — and need — a safe, quiet area to den, they don't automatically associate that area with the crate. After all, at first glance, it's not as inviting as that comfy couch in your living room. Nor is it always near you, which would be where they'd choose to spend their time if they could.

What that means is that you have to teach your dog that the crate is a *good* place. Fortunately, crate-training is pretty easy and requires only a few things, only one of which you have to shell out money for. Go to Chapter 3 for complete crate-training instructions and Chapter 4 for information on how to use the crate as a house-training tool.

The crate — duh

Crates come in a variety of styles and sizes. The most important thing is that you buy a crate that

- ✔ **Fits your dog:** The right size is one that lets your dog stand, turn around, and lie down comfortably, but isn't so big that your dog can eliminate in one end and then comfortably lie down without touching the poop or pee.

- ✔ **Serves the purposes you have intended for it:** Some crates are designed for light use — house-training puppies in the home, for example — while others are designed for car travel or air travel.

A crate is a big-ticket item, so shop aggressively. You can often find used ones at garage sales or in classified ads.

The right attitude

If you view the crate as a torture device, a punishment tool, or a way to get and keep your dog out of your hair, you won't be inclined to use it, or you'll be tempted to use it improperly.

During training, the crate is your tool. To make it an effective tool, you need to teach your dog that her crate is a good place to be and then you need to use the crate as outlined in Chapters 3 and 4. After the training is done (and if you decide to leave the crate available as a den for your dog), your dog decides when and whether to make use of it.

A training plan

The right crate-training plan is one that fosters positive associations with the crate, uses the crate to tap into your dog's natural instincts, and relies on routine (crate time balanced with family time) to help your dog learn acceptable behavior while still being an active member of your pack.

If used properly, you'll find that you go through stages with your crate. At first, you use it to house-train your dog and teach him your house rules. During this time, you'll confine your dog according to a schedule that ensures he gets potty time, mealtime, playtime, and crate time commensurate with his ability to hold his bladder. As his skill and control increase, his crate time decreases until, eventually, he's completely house-trained and a champion rule follower. At this point, the crate is there for his comfort only.

The Benefits of Crate-Training

A crate is probably the most versatile piece of dog gear ever made. Once used primarily for transporting dogs on airlines, the crate in all its varieties — open mesh, wire, or high-impact plastic — is now widely used and recognized as one of the best tools for making living with your pet easier. The following sections outline some of the key advantages crate-trained dogs and their owners have.

House-training goes more smoothly

Nothing makes the whole teaching-doggie-bathroom-manners process easier than having a crate that capitalizes on your dog's instinctive desire to keep her den clean. When you crate-train your dog, you keep your four-legged friend in her doggie den whenever you can't watch her directly and let her out for mealtimes, potty breaks, and playtime.

Being confined to a crate during house-training encourages your puppy to develop bladder control and decreases her opportunities to have accidents in the house. And putting her on a schedule establishes a routine that you and she will come to rely on years down the road.

It protects both dog and home

A crate is especially useful during the early stages of training when your dog or puppy doesn't know the house rules and is liable to bound happily from one potential trouble spot to another (electrical cords, vases on tables, small toys with easily swallowed parts, and more). If he's crate-trained, you can ensure his safety when you're gone or occupied with other things that make watching him difficult.

Crate-training can protect your possessions, too. An untrained and unsupervised dog can do quite a bit of damage. Not maliciously. Not with intent. But just because. She'll poop or pee on the foyer throw just because she had to go and this seemed like a perfectly suitable place. She'll chew the leg rungs on your dining room chairs just because she's a little bored and the resistance of the wood feels good against her teeth and gums. She'll explore the tiny little hole in the ottoman just because the fluff peaking through caught her eye — and the longer she explores, the more good stuff appears.

Traveling is safer and easier

The crate is perfect for its original purpose: transporting your pet. A loose dog in the car can be an annoyance — even a danger. Everyone is safer when crates are used. And talk about safety! In an automobile accident, a loose dog is as vulnerable as an unbelted human. Crates are tough, so much so that a crated dog once survived an airline crash with near-total human casualties.

When traveling with your pet, you'll find showing up with a crate will endear you to hotel owners, some of whom can be sweet-talked into lifting "no dog" rules if they know your dog will be crated in the room — as opposed to chewing up the bedspread.

Need another reason to crate-train your dog? In times of disaster — floods, earthquakes, hurricanes — a crate can save your pet's life by keeping him secure and providing you with alternatives if you have to evacuate your home. The cages of veterinary hospitals and animal shelters adjacent to a disaster area fill up quickly, but there's always room for the pet who brings his own shelter.

A Whirlwind Tour through the Positive Training Method

Punishment-based training methods have been around for a long time. Using these methods, you teach your dog that she can avoid punishment (pain or intimidation, for example) by doing what she's supposed to. In punishment-based training, dog owners use force — collar jerks, ear pinches, intimidation, and so on — to teach their dogs appropriate behavior. These methods certainly work, and you can find many trainers who swear by them.

Driving Miss Bailey: Travel crate alternatives

The safest way to transport your dog in a vehicle is in his crate. A loose dog in a car is a danger to you and your dog — having him in a crate protects both of you.

For some vehicles, such as sedans, crates are too large or cumbersome. A solution is a harness especially designed for dogs that works sort of like a car seat for a child. Secure the harness with the seatbelt and your dog can ride comfortably on the rear seat, either sitting up or lying down.

In a station wagon or SUV, another alternative is a dog barrier that separates the cargo area from the main cabin. Talk to your car dealer about this option.

The training instructions in this book, however, are based on the principles of *positive dog training* (also called *positive motivation dog training*). In this training method, you teach your dog that when he does good things (that is, what he's supposed to do), good things (praise, treats, rewards, and so on) happen; when he does bad things, the good things go away.

Like any dog-training technique, positive dog training requires you to be consistent and vigilant. Unlike traditional methods, however, it requires a shift in what you look for. Traditional methods rely on fear and submission; for these methods to work, you have to catch your dog being bad so that you can teach him the lesson: Don't do that again. Positive dog training requires that you catch your dog being good because the lesson here is: Do that again!

Here's how positive dog training works:

- ✔ **You reward your dog for behaving the way you want her to; then, because she's always on the lookout for rewards, she'll continue to repeat the desired behavior.** You associate the behavior with a *cue* (a movement or phrase) so that you can elicit the behavior on command. Eventually, when the behavior is ingrained in your dog, reduce the amount of rewards you give until you give them only occasionally.

- ✔ **You interrupt and redirect unwanted behaviors.** If your dog is chewing away happily on a sofa leg, interrupt that behavior by saying "no" in a quiet, low voice, and then making a sudden noise that startles her enough to look up at you. In that brief second when you have her attention, say "Good girl" (that's the praise you give her for stopping her attack on the sofa leg) and give her an alternative — her favorite chew toy, for example. If she caught you off-guard and you don't have an immediate alternative, keep her attention by making kissing noises and then redirect her to something more appropriate.

✔ **You withhold attention and rewards when your dog's doing something she's not supposed to.** Dogs repeat whatever behavior gets them attention. If your dog starts pawing and whining for you to let her in your lap, for example, look away with your chin up (this action is a dismissal thing) and ignore her until she settles down. *Then* you can stroke her (she's doing what you want — she stopped nagging) or put her in your lap.

Chapter 2

Choosing the Crate and Getting It Ready

• •

In This Chapter
▶ Choosing from a variety of crate styles
▶ Getting the right crate size
▶ Accessorizing your dog's crate

• •

Crates serve a number of very useful purposes (refer to Chapter 1 for a complete list) and can end up being a haven your dog chooses to retire to. Note that the preceding sentence deliberately uses the word can.

Crating your dog successfully depends on a couple of key factors: using it properly (the topic of Chapters 3 and 4) and choosing the right type and size.

Just as there's no one-size-fits-all house, there's no one-size-fits-all crate. You have to find one that's just the right size for your dog (neither too big nor too small) and that's designed for the purpose you intend it for.

Picking the Right Type of Crate

Crates come in all sorts of different sizes, materials, and colors. You can find a variety of crates in pet

stores, pet-supply stores, dog magazines, and sometimes at lawn-and-garden shops. Depending on the
style and manufacturer, expect to spend anywhere
from $40 to $200.

This section explains the benefits and drawbacks of a
variety of two crate types. Ultimately, which type of
crate to use is up to you. Just assess what your future
needs are likely to be and make an educated guess as
to which type of crate your dog will prefer.

 Most pet owners who use crates have a prefer-
ence. Some prefer plastic crates because of
the denlike qualities they provide. Others
prefer wire crates because they keep dogs
safely confined yet let the dogs see what's
going on around them. If you have a friend
who has a crate she's not using, ask to borrow
it. You may find that you really like that style
and can then confidently choose your own,
or you may discover that another style may
work better.

Plastic crates

Plastic crates, also known as carriers, are molded two-
piece units with doors at their fronts and ventilation at
their sides (see Figure 2-1).

Plastic crates offer several advantages:

✔ **They're ideal as an everyday crate in a well-
ventilated environment.** Because they're
enclosed on three sides (except for the vents),
plastic crates can easily become the snug, dark,
cozy dens most dogs crave.

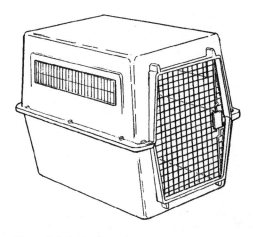

Figure 2-1: A plastic crate.
Illustration by Marcia Schlehr

A plastic crate may be the better choice in these situations:

- Your dog is easily distracted and bothered by outside noises and activity.

- Your dog is easily chilled. Because these crates are enclosed, they block drafts and tend to be cozier.

✔ **Plastic crates are standard for travel.** They work well for transporting your dog, especially if you have one who tends to bark at every signpost or pedestrian, or who just gets generally overstimulated by the passing scenery.

Plastic crates generally meet airline specifications for pet shipment as baggage or cargo — an important consideration if you plan to travel by air with your canine companion.

✔ **Plastic crates often cost a little less than wire crates do.**

Plastic crates do have their downsides, though:

✔ **They're big and bulky.** If you plan to use your crate only for training, at some point (when your dog is fully trained and completely trustworthy), you'll no longer need the crate. But they can take up more than a little storage space because they don't collapse or fold.

✔ **They're vulnerable to chewing.** The plastic makes these crates more vulnerable than wire crates to the ravages of canine teeth.

When you buy a crate, be sure that the latch works and the carrying handle is secure.

Wire crates

Wire crates are made from panels of welded metal wire that are hinged together (see Figure 2-2). Wire crates also have some advantages:

✔ **Their all-around openness allows your dog to see what's going on when he's lounging in his doggie abode.** If your dog doesn't like such openness, you can throw a blanket over the top and sides of the wire crate to create a more enclosed den.

✔ **Wire crates are totally collapsible.** So, you can stash them away in tiny places when you're not using them.

- ✔ **Wire crates are far easier to adjust for size than plastic crates are.** If you're choosing a crate for a small puppy who will one day grow into a large dog, you may prefer a more easily adjustable crate (for properly sizing a crate, see the later section "Sizing Up the Situation for Your Dog"). You can use dividers to size the crate to your puppy as she grows.

- ✔ **Wire crates allow for better air flow and offer more ventilation than plastic ones do.** If your pooch is a snub-nosed breed, such as a Pug or Boston Terrier, opt for a wire crate; such dogs are prone to breathing difficulties. Make sure to place the crate out of any potential drafts, however.

Figure 2-2: A wire crate.

Illustration by Marcia Schlehr

Like plastic crates, wire crates also carry a couple of disadvantages: They're not considered acceptable for airline travel (although you can set them up in your car for car travel), and they cost more than their plastic counterparts do.

> The most versatile crates have two doors, one on the side and one at the end. You'll appreciate this flexibility, especially when you have to move the crate from room to room.

Other types of crates

Plastic and wire crates are the most common, but there are other types of crates you can choose from:

✔ **Soft-sided crates:** In addition to plastic and wire crates, a third kind of carrier is available: a soft-sided crate. These carriers are lighter and easier to set up than plastic or wire crates and are often marketed as portable dog crates (see Figure 2-3).

Despite these benefits, soft-sided crates have these disadvantages:

- **They're not good for house-training,** especially puppies. The reason: Such crates can't withstand the ravages of canine teeth. Stick with a wire or plastic crate for in-home house-training.

- **They're not good for transporting your pet.** They're great for when you reach your destination, but they're not designed to be pet carriers.

✔ **Deluxe crates:** Incorporating a variety of materials (wood, wicker, and so on), these crates are both functional and attractive — and expensive. They're best for at-home use; consider another type if you plan to use your crate to transport your dog.

Figure 2-3: A soft-sided crate.

Sizing Up the Situation for Your Dog

The whole point behind crating your dog is to simulate the kind of environment he would happily choose for himself if he were still running wild with his ancestors. And his ancestors liked close, dark, cozy dens. The idea is that you can use your dog's denning instincts to your (and his) advantage.

The only caveat? You've got to get the size right. If the crate is too small, it's not a den — it's a cell, and he'll reject it. And if it's too large, it's a den and free space, and you've just undermined the one natural instinct you can use to make house-training easier: your dog's natural reluctance to soil his own living area.

To help you avoid falling into either trap, the following sections explain how to know when the size is right and what to do when you're buying a crate for a growing puppy.

The ideal size

You may think that bigger is usually better when it comes to houses, but that's not the case with dog crates. The crate shouldn't be so big that it invites your dog to divide it into a living area and a bathroom area, with enough room left over for a conversation pit. He just needs a crate that's big enough to allow him, at full size, to stand up without hitting his head, turn around without bumping into the sides, and lie down comfortably.

Different manufacturers make crates of different sizes. Some manufacturers list specific dimensions; others specify sizes that go anywhere from extra-small to extra-large. If you need help determining which size will be best for your dog, ask a salesclerk for help.

When you're buying a crate for a puppy

Picking the right size crate for your dog is crucial — but just what is the right size when your dog isn't yet fully grown?

Fortunately, you don't have to keep buying new crates for each growth spurt your puppy has. The right size crate is one your puppy will fit comfortably in when she's full grown. So if you have a puppy who will one day grow into a 150-pound Great Dane, buy an extra-large crate. If your darling is likely to get no bigger than a 6-pound Chihuahua, a small crate is just fine.

You can actually buy one crate that can serve as your dog's den from puppyhood on. The secret: Buy an adult-sized wire crate and block off some of the inside space while your dog is a puppy. Many wire crates come with dividers, wire panels that are similar to the plates at the back of the drawers in metal file cabinets. You simply slide the divider back as your puppy grows and needs a bigger crate. The budget-friendly result is that you have to buy only one crate for your dog's lifetime. Another alternative is to put a big cardboard box at one end of a plastic crate (upside down so that your dog can't crawl in). Just decrease the box size as your puppy grows.

Readying Your Dog's Home within a Home

You want your dog's crate to be inviting and comfortable. Fortunately, for a canine, inviting is pretty easy to do. A soft place to rest and a couple of toys to keep her occupied are about all it takes. Of course, you can add a little more, but you don't need to. The following sections explain.

Lining the bottom with comfy bedding

Crate manufacturers make a variety of mats and carpets to fit their products, including luxurious items such as cut-to-fit mats made of synthetic sheepskin and more basic (but still very comfortable) plastic polyure-thane foam mats.

Of course, you don't have to buy specially made bed-ding from a manufacturer. You can use anything that is soft and comfortable, won't easily shred, or isn't already coming apart. An old baby blanket or towel is perfectly fine, and so is an old pillow that's had so many heads resting on it that it already has a nice hollow that a dog can curl up in.

When you're deciding on bedding, keep these things in mind:

✔ **Use bedding that's washable.** You can throw baby blankets and towels into the wash. If you use an actual pillow or dog bed, make sure it has removable, washable slipcovers, or is itself machine-washable.

✔ **Pay attention to size.** If you're lining the crate, don't cram it full of bedding. You want your dog to be able to move around freely, not fight the bedding for a good spot to lie down.

 A dog is less likely to chew on the bedding if she has other more appropriate things to chew on. Be sure to put in a chewie or some other toy that'll keep her busy and happy while she's in her crate. The next section has suggestions.

✔ **Don't go with too much fluff or any frills.** Avoid fluffy beds or cushions because both can encour-age chewing or accidents.

✔ **Watch for shredding.** If your puppy chews on her bedding, be sure to check it regularly for shred-ding. Then simply trim off the long ends when you find them.

Tossing in a couple of toys

If you don't provide your dog (especially a puppy) with toys, he'll find his own, like your heirloom pillows or the gerbil you let roam in a plastic bubble. So make sure you put at least one or two of the following toys in your dog's crate:

- ✔ **Chew toys:** Any toy made of hard rubber can satisfy your puppy's need to chew. You can find hard chews in various shapes — bones, little critters, balls, and so on.

- ✔ **Love-y toys:** Many dogs like cuddling and carrying around small stuffed animals.

 When you look for dog toys, make sure that they don't have any small, detachable pieces that your dog can swallow, no wires he can get caught up in, and no holes for stuffing to come out of. Any of these things can pose a health hazard to your dog.

Adding a "security blanket" if needed

Some puppies feel acutely lonely when they're separated from everything they know. If your puppy has been recently separated from her mother and siblings, consider adding to her crate an item (like a towel or toy) from her life with her breeder. The familiar smell may help her through the first few days and ease the transition to her new digs.

If you have an adult dog who suffers from a little separation anxiety, the same trick can help him when he's confined while you're at work or kenneled during your vacation.

Severe separation anxiety is a real problem, and dogs who suffer from it may bark incessantly, scratch frantically at doors, and chew destructively, even to the point of harming themselves. If your dog displays these behaviors, contact your vet or trainer about strategies you can use to help relieve the anxiety.

Chapter 3

A Step-by-Step Guide to Successfully Crate-Training Your Dog

. . . .

In This Chapter

▶ Following the complete crate-training instructions

▶ Getting your dog to sleep through the night in his crate

▶ Avoiding over-crating your dog

. . . .

C rate-training your dog provides peace of mind for you and a safe place for your dog when she wants some peace and quiet and to get away from the hubbub of family life.

How successful you are at getting your dog to like and willingly use the crate, however, depends almost entirely on how you go about training her to it. You probably already know that you're just setting yourself up for failure if your approach is simply to force her in or leave her for hours on end. But there are other, more innocuous ways you can foster negative associations with the crate: using it only when you're leaving, for example, or only when you're frustrated and want her out of your hair. Fortunately, the right strategy for crate-training is really easy. It just takes a little time and patience and a plan. This chapter explains.

Crate Training, Easy as 1-2-3

Okay, crate-training takes a few more than three steps, but it *is* easy. To help your dog appreciate his crate, introduce him to it immediately but gradually. If possible, start on the very same day you welcome him into your home. The entire process should take only a day or two, unless your four-legged friend has had a prior negative experience with the crate. If that's the case with your dog, expect the process to take longer.

The key is just to go *s-l-o-w-l-y* and be patient. If, at any point in the process outlined in the following sections, your dog starts to whine or cry, you may be moving too quickly.

 Your dog won't like the arrangement at first and won't hesitate to let you know how unhappy he is, but he'll eventually get used to, and even begin to enjoy, his quiet time. In fact, after he's trained and roaming the house freely, don't be surprised to find him napping or resting in his crate of his own free will.

 During the day and early evening, the ideal place for your dog's crate is in a quiet, out-of-the-way place in the main living area, where she can still see and hear you, even though she won't be in the thick of the action. If you spend almost as much time in your kitchen as you do in the living room, try putting the crate in a place where the puppy can see both areas.

Step 1: Tie one on — The open-door policy

You need to make the crate, particularly the door, non-threatening to your four-legged friend. A door that suddenly slams shut while your dog is getting accustomed to the crate can spook your pooch into bypassing the crate completely.

Step 2: Encourage exploration

As your new pup explores your house (with you trailing close behind to keep her out of trouble), chances are, she'll find the crate you lovingly set up and prepared for her (refer to Chapter 3 for guidance on that). If you're introducing a crate to a dog who's already part of your household, you need to let her explore in much the same way.

Begin by letting her walk around the crate to sniff and otherwise explore it. If she hesitates, throw little treats around the perimeter.

Step 3: Lure her in

When your puppy approaches the crate comfortably, see whether you can induce her to venture inside the crate — with the help of a tasty treat, if necessary. If your house-trainee isn't food-motivated, a favorite toy may do the trick. Either way, toss the treat or toy inside the crate. If she goes in readily, praise her; if she's hesitant, tell her in a high, happy-sounding voice to go and get the goodies.

Don't force her in — let her decide on her own to enter the crate. And when she does, let her know what a good girl she is. This may take some time; be prepared to spend an afternoon or so helping her with this crucial step.

Whenever your puppy enters the crate (or whenever you put her in it), use a word that tells her what she's doing and where she's going. Good choices are *crate, place, bed,* or any other word that you know you'll use consistently. By saying this same word in a high, happy tone of voice whenever your dog enters her crate, you'll help her associate the word with the crate — and she'll soon begin to head into the crate as soon as you, well, say the word.

Step 4: Shut the door (but not for long)

If your puppy repeatedly enters her crate without hesitation, untie the door and toss a treat inside the crate. When your pooch enters, shut the door quietly without locking it. Leave it shut for just a few seconds.

During those few seconds, praise your pooch lavishly, and then open the door and coax her out. Another tiny treat should provide sufficient incentive for her to emerge.

Perform this sequence five to ten times during the day, gradually increasing the amount of time the door remains closed, until your puppy is able to remain calmly in the crate for about five minutes.

Step 5: Leave the room

After your puppy can stay calmly in the crate for five minutes, you're ready for the next step, which is to have him stay calmly in his crate without you there. Once again, lure your pooch into his crate — but this time, use something more substantial than a treat or two. A full meal dispensed into a crate dish is a good choice (see Figure 3-1).

Place his bowl in front of the crate and let him eat. The next time you feed him, place the food just inside the crate. With every successive meal, put the bowl farther inside the crate until it's at the far end. When your pup is in his crate, shut the door quietly and leave the room for about a minute. When you return, see what your puppy's doing. If he's eating his meal or gnawing his chew toy contentedly, leave the room again and come back in a few more minutes. Keep checking until he's finished; when he's done, let him out of the crate and praise him lavishly for his accomplishment. Give him a special treat to emphasize to him how pleased you are.

Then with each successive feeding, increase the length of time you leave him in his crate with the door closed.

Figure 3-1: Feeding a puppy in a crate.
Photo by Jack and Wendy Volhard

An alternative is to use a food-stuffed toy — see the sidebar titled "No dishes? No problem!" for details.

No dishes? No problem!

Maybe your dog's crate doesn't come with dishes, or maybe you just find them too cumbersome, messy, or awkward to use. That's okay. You have another option for keeping your dog occupied while she's in the crate: filling an interactive toy with food and/or treats.

Take a toy such as a Kong (you can find one at any pet-supply store) or other food-dispensing plaything and slather some peanut butter on the inside. Then fill the toy with treats, or even regular food, and pack it tight. Put the stuffed toy inside your pooch's crate. Chances are, she'll make a beeline for the toy, get immediately to work trying to ferret out the goodies you've shoe-horned into it, and not even notice that you've closed the door.

This trick works not only for crate training but also for other training situations. For example, dogs with separation anxiety often do very well if their owners give them food-stuffed inter-active toys just before they leave the house. The dogs are so engrossed in getting the goodies that they don't even realize their people have left — and afterward, their contented tummies may well induce them to take a post-snacking nap.

Of course, if you make a regular practice of giving your pooch a meal in one of her toys, make sure you adjust her other meal portions accordingly. That way, she'll retain her girlish figure as she works her way to becoming a house-training graduate.

Step 6: Build up her tolerance

You're now ready for the final step in your puppy's Loving the Crate 101 course: building up her tolerance for being in the crate by herself. This one should be easy: Keep feeding her inside the crate until she's able to stay in it for half an hour.

Then try leaving the house for a few minutes, gradually extending the time that you're away. At this point, she should handle crate time without any problem.

Step 7: Keep crate love alive

 You need to do your part to make sure that the crate continues to be something your dog loves. Here are some ways to do just that:

✔ **Potty first.** If you plan to have your puppy or dog stay in his crate while you leave the house, give him an opportunity to poop or pee beforehand. A before-the-crate bathroom break greatly decreases the odds that your four-legged friend will go to the bathroom while he's in the crate.

✔ **Let him settle.** If you're crating your puppy or dog in his crate while you go out to run errands, put him there a few minutes before you depart. That way, he'll have a chance to settle himself before you head out the door.

✔ **Downplay comings and goings.** Don't make a big deal of putting your dog in his crate when you leave or of letting him out when you arrive home. Big, emotional hellos and goodbyes can put your dog on emotional overload, making settling down in the crate tougher for him to accomplish.

✔ **Potty last.** Just as you took him to his potty before you left, do the same thing when you arrive home. A dog who's held his poop and pee while crated needs and deserves the consideration of a bathroom break as soon as possible thereafter.

Silly kids! Crates are for dogs!

Remember those commercials for Trix cereal in which a rabbit kept trying to eat the cereal, only to be told, "Silly rabbit! Trix are for kids"? Well, when it comes to kids and crates, the opposite is true: "Silly kids! Crates are for dogs!"

Unfortunately, most children have difficulty grasping this concept, at least initially. Particularly if the crate in question holds a large dog, most children consider it to be a brand-new indoor playhouse. They just can't seem to resist crawling into the crate, either to play in it by themselves or to share some one-on-one time with Fido.

You should do your very best to discourage this practice. Tell your kids that the crate is Fido's own private space and that he shouldn't be expected to share that space with anyone else. And explain, too, that they shouldn't try to play with Fido when he's in his crate. Crate time is downtime for dogs, just as naptime or bedtime is downtime for children.

Solving Common Crate-Training Problems

Alas, not every dog appreciates a crate. An adult dog who's never been inside a crate may think it's a prison, not a haven. A puppy-mill pooch who spent his baby-hood cramped inside a crate that was too small and who was forced to eliminate while inside that crate may not think the crate you've purchased is such a great idea, either.

The following list explains how to approach — and hopefully solve — common problems:

- ✔ **If your dog is hesitant and/or resistant to going inside the crate:** A dog who hesitates to enter a crate for the first time probably just needs some patience from you and a clear incentive to give the crate a try. Find a treat that your dog is passionate about and hold it to her nose so that she knows what's being offered. Then use a high-pitched, happy-sounding tone of voice to encourage her to enter the crate. As soon as she makes the big step and ventures inside the crate, praise her to the skies. Above all, don't shut the door until she's going in and out of the crate without hesitation.

- ✔ **If your dog goes into the crate willingly, but soon thereafter whines to be let out:** He may simply be bored. Be sure to give him something fun to keep him occupied when you leave. Interactive toys stuffed with treats, or a Kong with treats inside, are a wonderful way to make the crate fun. Also, active dogs can't release their abundant energy in a crate. When he's not in the crate, make sure he gets enough exercise to run off the extra energy so that he *can* rest once confined.

- ✔ **If your dog balks the first time you leave her alone in the crate:** If that's the case with your pooch, stay away for just a minute or so after she starts fussing. Then come back into the room and reassure her with a quick "good girl" or "good dog." Leave the room again for just a few seconds — and if she stays quiet for that brief time, come back to let her out of the crate and praise her. The important thing here is not to let her out of the crate until she stops fussing; otherwise, you teach her that whining is the way to open the door.

✔ **If your dog suffers from separation anxiety:**
A dog who suffers from separation anxiety — in other words, panics and becomes destructive when left alone — can benefit from professional help. An experienced trainer can help you teach your anxious pooch that solitude is okay. In severe cases, a veterinarian can prescribe medication that helps to lessen the dog's anxiety.

If you've done your best but there's no way your dog will accept the crate, don't despair. For a few pooches, the crate will never be the cozy den it represents to the vast majority of canines. For these dogs, the solution is to create an indoor home-alone area that's less enclosed than a crate is but still protects your home while the dogs learn proper potty protocol.

It's 11 O'Clock: Do You Know Where Your Dog Is?

Whether you have a puppy you're trying to house-train or an adult dog who isn't quite ready for the freedom to roam your house at will, you'll crate her at night. For a dog who's used to the crate, crating is just part of the nighttime routine. You say the word — *crate, bedtime,* or whatever other term you chose to use to indicate crate-time — and she docilely walks to her bed and snuggles down for the night.

Alas, puppies recently removed from their mothers are not quite so amenable. During the first couple of nights at her new home, the reassuring warmth of her littermates is gone and everything has changed. She's going to have a lot to say about this, so be prepared. She'll fuss less if she's in your presence and can be reassured by your smell and the sound of your breathing.

 Follow these steps to help your puppy make it through these first nights in her new home:

1. **Set up her crate next to your bed, and prepare it with a soft blanket to sleep on and a chew toy or two.**

2. **Firmly tell her "crate" (or whatever word you use to indicate it's crate-time), put her inside, and close the door.**

   And then open a book, because you won't be sleeping for a while. Many young puppies object to being put in crates at night during their first few nights in a new home. They cry pitifully and otherwise carry on, tempting their soft-hearted people to scoop them out of their crates and allow them to sleep with them in their own beds.

3. **Endure the cries and whines as best you can.**

   Try dangling your fingers. For a few people-loving puppies, being in their humans' bedrooms doesn't offer enough proximity to their humans. If that's the case with your new four-legged friend, bring his crate right up next to your bed and dangle your fingers in front of the crate door every time he cries. Chances are, he'll sniff your fingers and quiet down.

 Here's what you don't want to do:

✔ **Don't punish your puppy.** Scolding your puppy, using a shake can, banging on the crate, or issuing any other negative response to his whining usually won't keep him quiet — or if it does, not for very long. Staying positive helps him associate the crate with pleasant occurrences.

✔ **Don't take her out when she's carrying on.** If you do, you're setting yourself up for multiple heartrending performances and teaching her that the way to get out is to fuss loudly enough.

She'll probably settle down and then wake once or twice in the middle of the night.

4. **If she wakes up during the night, take her out to relieve herself — and praise her for doing so — and then put her back in her crate.**

Most puppies younger than 4 months can't hold it all night long. Take a look at what time it is: If your puppy's whining any time after 2 a.m. or so, and several hours have passed since his previous pit stop, haul yourself out of bed and take him to his potty spot.

Don't let him linger and don't engage in playtime.

In a day or two, the worst of the heartbreaking crying is over, and you'll both be sleeping better.

Timely Matters: Be Reasonable!

Say you love your comfy chair. It's in a perfect spot in your living room, it has your favorite cuddly blanket and perfect lighting for reading; plus, you can see the TV unobstructed. You go to it willingly whenever you want to relax, right? Now suppose that, for no apparent reason and without any warning, you're frequently forced to stay in that chair for hours on end without relief. Chances are, you'd lose some of your affection for it.

Same with your dog and her crate. Too much of a good thing quickly turns bad. If you want your dog to continue to see her crate as a refuge and to not object when it's time to go in, don't make the number-one mistake people make with crates: keeping their dogs in them for too long.

Limiting crate time

With crate-training, you keep your four-legged friend in her doggie den whenever you can't watch her directly and let her out for mealtimes, potty breaks, and play-time. Nothing makes the whole process of teaching doggie bathroom manners easier than having a crate that capitalizes on your dog's instinctive desire to keep her den clean.

But that said, it's entirely possible that use of a crate can be too much of a good thing — and even cruel to your four-legged friend.

Too many people embrace the crate a little too tightly and turn it into a canine warehouse. They put their dogs into their crates in the morning, go out all day, and then come home in the evening to let their pooches out. Yes, the furniture and rugs are free of destruction, dog poop, and other hazards that are part of sharing one's life with a dog. But confining your dog to a crate for that long is inhumane — even if she can hold it all day.

Not only does crating your dog for too long cause her discomfort in bowel and bladder — possibly even causing a urinary tract infection — but you also deprive your dog of exercise, mental stimulation, and your company, all of which can cause her to develop a distaste for her crate. And if she can't hold her poop and pee, you've really made things tough for her, because you've forced her to dirty her den and then stay in that dirt until you let her out.

How long can you ultimately leave your dog in his crate unattended? That depends on your dog and your schedule. Here are some general guidelines:

✔ **For fully house-trained dogs:** Don't confine them to a crate for more than four or five hours at a time.

 Make fresh water available at all times during the day. If your dog will be in his crate for more than two hours, leave him a dish of fresh water in the crate. You also can attach a little water bucket to the inside of the crate. After 8 p.m., remove his water dish so he can last through the night without having to make a trip outside.

✔ **For dogs who are still being house-trained:** A puppy's ability to control elimination increases with age, at the rate of about one hour per month. Until he's 6 months of age, don't expect a puppy to last for more than four hours during the day without having to eliminate.

That said, it's okay to crate a dog overnight after she's demonstrated that she can hold it for that long (generally after a puppy reaches 4 months of age).

If you have a female puppy and you notice frequent urinary accidents, it could be a sign of a bladder infection called *cystitis*. A trip to the vet can confirm and treat this condition.

Managing breaks when you're gone all day

If you think your schedule or your home décor requires all-day crate confinement for your dog, you need to explore other options, several of which are outlined in the following bullet list.

If none of the following options for relieving your home-alone dog are available five days a week, maybe you can combine them: work from home one or two days a week, go home for lunch one or two days a week, ask a neighbor for help one or two days a week, or try some other combination.

✔ **Get a pet sitter or dog walker.** Dog owners who reside in major metropolitan areas or their surrounding suburbs can find plenty of qualified pet sitters, dog walkers, or pet-sitting companies by logging on to an online classified Web site such as craigslist (www.craigslist.org) or by visiting the Web site of Pet Sitters International (www.petsit.com/locate) or the National Association of Professional Pet Sitters (www.petsitters.org). Or enlist the assistance of a dog-loving neighbor who's home during the day.

✔ **Bring your dog to work.** Many companies allow employees to bring their dogs to work with them; maybe yours is one.

✔ **Go home for lunch.** If your workplace is close to your home and you have an hour or so for lunch, consider going home at lunchtime and taking your pooch out for a potty break. Eat lunch at your desk either before or after the trip.

✔ **Work from home.** Maybe your job allows you to telecommute, at least temporarily. If you spend most of your workday in front of a computer and/or on the phone, see whether your company allows you to work from home, at least during your canine companion's house-training stage.

✔ **Consider doggie day care.** More and more cities and towns offer cage-free doggie day care to give the confined canine a more pleasurable day. These day cares work pretty much like child day cares: You drop off your dog in the morning and pick him up after work.

To find a doggie day care in your area, look online, in the phone book, or in the newspaper's classified ads, or talk to a friend who uses such a service or to your vet for recommendations.

Chapter 4

Using the Crate to House-Train Your Dog

●●●●●●●●●●●●●●●●●●●●●●●●●●●●●●●●

In This Chapter

▶ Finding basic principles to guide your house-training efforts

▶ Following instructions for both indoor and outdoor house-training

▶ Solving common house-training problems

●●●●●●●●●●●●●●●●●●●●●●●●●●●●●●●●

A visit to any animal shelter provides heart-rending evidence of what happens when the bond between dog and person is broken. One common cause of a rupture in the bond between a dog and his person is the dog's bathroom behavior. In a study sponsored by the National Council on Pet Population Study & Policy (www.petpopulation.org), house-soiling was the most common reason that owners surrendered their dogs to shelters when those owners cited a variety of reasons for relinquishing their dogs.

This doesn't have to happen. A little time, a little patience, and a little perseverance can get just about any dog to become a house-training ace. Make that investment in your dog's future, and you up the odds that the two of you will have a long and happy life together.

Professional dog trainers and experienced dog owners have dealt with a lot of puppy pee and doggie doo. Not surprisingly, they've gotten house-training down to a science. And just about every one of them will tell you that using a crate makes house-training easier, quicker, and more effective than any other method.

House-Training Basics

To know whether your dog is really house-trained, you need to understand exactly what house-training is. Simply put, *house-training* is the process in which you teach your dog to eliminate when and where you want him to — and to refrain from eliminating at any other time or place.

That definition doesn't allow much room for errors or lapses. And clearly, when measured against those criteria, a dog who consistently does his duty where he's supposed to (outdoors or in a designated indoor area) is fully house-trained, and those who don't aren't. House-training is one of those all-or-nothing cases.

To increase the likelihood that your dog will graduate house-training school with honors, put the principles outlined in the following sections into action.

Use a crate

Until your dog is fully house-trained, she shouldn't have access to your entire home unless you can be right there to watch her every move. If you don't watch what your four-legged friend is doing, you won't see when she performs a doggie download — and you'll miss what educators call a *teachable moment:* the opportunity to teach your canine companion where she should do her business.

But, of course, no one can watch a dog 24/7. That's why, during the times you can't cast an eagle eye on your canine companion, she needs to be confined, ideally to a crate which, because of your dog's reluctance to soil it, helps her gain more control of her bladder, a key requirement to putting her on a potty schedule.

Confining your dog to a crate teaches her patience and control. Because she doesn't want to soil her sleeping area, she'll wait to go to the bathroom until you let her out. It's an effective house-training tool because it taps into your dog's natural behavior — or what she would do in the wild without you around to encourage her to make good choices.

Most domestic dogs do just about anything to avoid peeing or pooping in their dens. When that den is a crate, a dog learns to hold her pee and poop whenever she's inside. If possible, she lets her floodgates open only when she's away from these cherished structures of safety. Sounds simple, doesn't it?

Using a crate to potty-train your dog is simple, but it's not quite effortless. You can't just run out, buy a crate, and shove your dog into it with the idea that you'll house-train her at warp speed. You still need to actively train her.

Choosing the right spot: Outdoor training

Outdoor training involves teaching a dog to eliminate in a potty area located outside your home. The potty area can be a designated spot in your backyard or wherever you allow your dog to do his business.

Outdoor training has plenty of advantages. First and foremost, as soon as your dog knows what he's supposed to do and where he's supposed to do it, you never again need to worry about canine waste marring your floors, staining your carpets, or otherwise stinking up your house. And those who choose to walk their dogs outdoors can get some healthful, enjoyable exercise, as well as some special bonding time with their canine companions.

But outdoor training carries some disadvantages, too — just ask anyone who's had to go outside with his pooch on a cold or rainy night.

Avoiding the elements: Indoor training

Indoor training involves teaching a dog to eliminate in a potty area located inside your home. The potty area can be some newspapers spread on the floor in one room, a litter box tucked discreetly into a corner, or some other device located in a designated area of your abode.

A dog who's indoor-trained makes a beeline for that indoor location whenever he feels the urge to eliminate. As soon as he's finished, cleanup is easy: You just flush the poop down the toilet and either throw away or clean the surface upon which the poop or pee landed.

But indoor training carries some disadvantages. It's impractical if your dog is much bigger than toy-sized (consider how big that waste is likely to be). Moreover, if your canine companion is male, sooner or later he'll probably starting lifting his leg when he pees. When that happens, his ability to aim accurately may decline. Instead of hitting the litter box, newspaper, or other toilet, he may leave a stinky puddle on your floor.

Pick a type of indoor potty

If you opt for an indoor potty, you need to decide which type of indoor potty to use. Here are your options:

- ✔ **Newspapers:** Newspapers are cheap and readily available. What could be simpler? Their main drawback? The pee can soak through the paper to the floor underneath. To protect your floor, place an old shower curtain under the newspapers and use only the sections printed on newsprint; the slick, glossy color sections aren't absorbent at all. Be aware, however, that dogs tend to think that any type of paper is newspaper and will go on various papers you leave around the house.

- ✔ **Puppy training pads:** These pads, also known as *pee pads* or *pee-pee pads,* are made of absorbent layers of paper that are backed by a layer of plastic and are sealed around the edges. Because the pads are absorbent, a puddle is less likely to soak through the floor than with newspapers and is easier to clean up.

- ✔ **Litter boxes:** Similar to litter boxes that cats use, doggie litter boxes control pet waste odors and protect your floor. The boxes themselves have walls on three sides, and the fourth side is open to allow easy entry, and the main ingredients in the litter are recycled paper and/or wood pulp. (Don't use cat litter in dog litter boxes. Cat litter isn't designed to absorb doggie waste.)

- ✔ **Grate/tray potties:** These relatively new pooch potties come in two parts: an easy-to-clean plastic tray and a plastic grate that you place atop the tray. You don't need to buy anything else. But they can be cumbersome to clean up, depending on their size. That clumsiness of cleanup is also a reason not to use these potties for dogs who weigh more than 30 pounds.

Ways to improving house-training success

Most dog trainers say that the most important part of their jobs isn't training dogs — it's training the humans to train the dogs. You and the other humans in your life play crucial roles in your dog's house-training progress and ultimate success (or lack thereof). Not only do you teach your dog the ins and outs of proper potty protocol, but you also create the conditions that can make or break a house-training program. For one thing, house-training needs to be a family affair. Here's why:

✔ **To keep the diet consistent:** No matter how diligently you're trying to regulate Sparky's bathroom urges by regulating the kind and amount of food you feed him, such diligence is all for naught if your partner or child is sneaking the dog snacks all the while.

✔ **To help you avoid burnout:** House-training can be pretty simple, but it can also be pretty tedious when just one person is doing the day-in, day-out routine of feeding, walking, and confining the house-trainee.

Take into Account the Training Your Dog Has Already Had

You can housetrain almost any dog, but the challenges of teaching a puppy to go potty may differ from those you encounter when you try to teach the same maneuvers to an adult dog. Some of that has to do with the kind of nurturing and training the dog has already received.

The wee ones: Preliminary training and physical limits

All a healthy puppy usually needs to become house-trained is some time to grow and to develop some self-control — and, of course, some guidance from you in the meantime.

One crucial lesson she's only just starting to learn is the lesson of self-control. To put it simply, your little pup just can't hold it — at least not for very long. A puppy younger than 4 months doesn't have a big enough bladder or sufficient muscle control to go more than a couple of hours without eliminating. As she gets older, a pup's ability to control herself gradually increases. By the time she reaches adulthood at about 1 year of age, a healthy dog usually has plenty of self-control. In fact, some adult dogs can hold it for a *very* long time.

Before your young puppy can reliably control his bladder or bowel, you want to make sure *you* give him the access he needs to the appropriate bathroom area. Until your puppy is old enough to begin controlling his bathroom urges (usually around 8 weeks), you're not really house-training; you're avoiding accidents. Only when he begins to have some control over his bladder and bowel can you begin house-training in earnest.

Grown-up pooches: Unlearning bad habits

Even an adult dog who appears to have an iron bladder isn't necessarily house-trained. The fact that she *can* hold it doesn't necessarily mean that she *will* hold it or that she knows where to go to *do* it. An adult dog may be burdened with mental baggage or just plain bad habits that can create additional obstacles to house-training.

Not surprisingly, then, house-training an adult dog is often less straightforward than house-training a puppy. The grown-up pooch who has less-than-stellar bathroom manners often needs to unlearn some bad but well-entrenched habits before learning new ones. The person who lives with such a dog may need to develop his detective skills and figure out why his canine companion keeps making bathroom mistakes.

In any case, though, when you know something about your canine friend's instincts and impulses, you have a leg up on your efforts to house-train her.

Outdoor Training for Your Puppy

Outdoor training is the process of teaching your dog to eliminate only when she's outside. You can consider your pooch to be successfully outdoor-trained if she consistently holds her poop and pee until you take her outside — or if she takes herself there.

Achieving such success can be surprisingly simple. Every time you think your dog needs a potty break, you take her outside to her potty spot to do her business. At first, you do this according to a set schedule. Sometimes, though, your dog needs to diverge from that schedule — and in all likelihood, she'll communicate somehow that she needs to go.

At all other times, you either confine her to her crate or watch her continuously for those pre-potty communications. Your objective is to prevent accidents from occurring and to encourage your dog to do her business outdoors — and outdoors only. Within a matter of weeks, she understands that it's okay to potty outside and takes it upon herself to make sure that she doesn't eliminate inside.

Outdoor training doesn't have to be difficult, but it does require time, attention, and patience from you. Training puppies takes a little more work than training an adult dog — for one thing, puppies need more potty breaks — but either way, you can introduce your dog to his potty spot, set up a schedule, and get training off to a good start.

Going out to the potty spot

The way you behave while your dog potties can either speed up or slow down his outdoor house-training progress. That's because puppies have very short attention spans, and they can have a hard time staying focused during their potty breaks. Your behavior can either help your little guy get down to business or make him forget to do his business.

 To help your puppy concentrate on bathroom activities and get him thinking about those activities before you reach the potty spot, do the following:

✔ **As the two of you head out to your pup's bathroom, ask him, "Do you want to go potty?" or announce to him, "It's potty time!" in a lively, can't-wait-to-get-out-there tone.** Use the same expression and same tone of voice every time you take the little guy out, and soon he'll associate both with heading out to the bathroom.

✔ **Take the fastest, most direct route to the potty area, and use the same route every time your puppy needs a bathroom break.** Your consistency conditions your dog to expect that when he treads that path, he's going to eliminate shortly thereafter.

As you go to the potty spot, make sure you don't walk him anywhere near the mailbox or your prize rhododendron. The dog should not be allowed to pee just anywhere, particularly in the house-training process. Even after your dog is house-trained, if you're walking him outside, keep him off other people's lawns and confine his bathroom activities to the median strip between the sidewalk and street.

Have treats at the ready — in your coat pocket, in a small dish from which you can grab one or two — so you'll be able to give your puppy one of those treats while the two of you are outdoors. It's important to reward him immediately after he does his good deed so that he associates the reward with the deed.

Letting your pup do his business

When the two of you arrive at the potty spot, don't do anything. Don't talk to your puppy and don't play with him until he's figured out where he's going to go and is clearly about to do so. Let him walk around a little bit — no farther than the length of a 6-foot leash — and don't let him leave the area until he's unloaded.

As your little guy squats (male puppies don't start lifting their legs to pee until they're older, and most females never do), give him a command such as "Go potty" or "Do your business." Repeat this phrase every time he eliminates. By doing so, you up your puppy's chances of learning to pee and poop on command — a handy skill for him to have.

As soon as your puppy is finished, praise him for his performance in a high, happy-sounding voice (but don't get too loud, or you may scare the little guy). Give him a very small treat, take him for a walk, play with him, and indulge in a love fest. You've both earned it!

What if he doesn't go?

Sometimes, a puppy just won't eliminate — even though you think it's time for him to do some doo. If you've been out for more than five minutes and your puppy hasn't pooped or peed, take him back inside. But watch him like a hawk; don't take your eyes off him. Look for signs that he needs to go: circling, pacing, intense sniffing, a sudden stop in the middle of an activity. The second you see any such signs, get him back outside. If you can't watch him, put him in his crate.

Whether he's in his crate or out on the floor with you, take him out again after 20 minutes. If he goes, praise him, treat him, and take him back inside for some supervised playtime. If he doesn't go, put him back in his crate, wait another 20 minutes or so, and head back outside. Eventually he *will* go; he can't hold that poop or pee forever. Praise him lavishly and give him a teensy treat when he finally does unload.

Setting up a puppy potty schedule

Putting your puppy on a regular potty schedule can shorten his house-training learning curve considerably. Your pup, even at his young age, is a creature of habit. He learns through repetition. If you take him out to pee and poop at the same times each and every day, his body will become accustomed to that schedule. He'll be conditioned to do his business at the times you want him to do it.

 When you put together a potty schedule for your puppy, keep in mind that most juvenile canines need to poop and/or pee at the following times:

✔ First thing in the morning

✔ Last thing at night

✔ During the night (if the puppy is under 4 months of age)

✔ After energetic playing

✔ After being confined in a crate

✔ After a nap

✔ After chewing on a toy or a bone

✔ A few minutes after eating

Armed with this knowledge, along with your observations of your dog's individual potty pattern, you can create a schedule that gives your puppy enough time to pee or poop and also gives you some predictability.

A canine youngster who's under 3 or 4 months of age just can't hold his poop or pee for the entire night any more than a human infant can sleep through the night without filling his diaper. So when your puppy fidgets, whines, or cries in the middle of night, know that he probably has a very good reason to do so. Heed his plea and take him out.

Know that as your puppy gets older, he won't need to go outside in the middle of the night. The same will be true of the midmorning, midafternoon, and 7 p.m. pit stops, as well as the noontime feeding.

Outdoor Training for Adult Dogs

Teaching an adult dog to do her bathroom business outside is similar to teaching a puppy. The difference between the two is that the adult dog doesn't need nearly as many bathroom breaks as a puppy does. But the principles and procedures are the same: showing your four-legged friend that her bathroom is outside and doing whatever it takes to keep her from eliminating inside.

Table 4-1 shows a sample schedule for outdoor-training an adult dog. As soon as your adult dog has mastered her house-training basics — which can happen in just a few days — you can eliminate the noontime potty break and consider giving her a little more freedom in your home.

Table 4-1	A House-Training Schedule for an Adult Dog
Time	**Tasks**
7 a.m.	Get up.
	Take dog outside.
	Feed dog.
	Offer water.
	Take dog outside.
	Play with dog up to 15 minutes.
	Put dog in crate.
Noon	Take dog outside.
	Offer water.
	Play with dog 15 to 30 minutes.
	Put dog in crate.
5:30 p.m.	Take dog outside.
	Feed dog.
	Offer water.
	Play with dog for 1 hour and/or let her hang out with the family in the kitchen.
7 p.m.	Remove water.

Time	Tasks
Before bed	Take dog outside.
	Put dog in crate.

Indoor Training for Your Dog

The first and most important step to house-training your dog to use an indoor potty is to help her make the connection between the potty place and what she's supposed to do in that place. To do that, follow these steps:

1. **As soon as you and your new pet arrive home, take her to her indoor potty.**

   The car ride home often prompts a dog to eliminate immediately after the ride is over. If she hesitates to use the potty, lure her onto it or into it with a small treat.

2. **When she opens her floodgates and/or makes a solid deposit, praise her lavishly and give her a tiny treat.**

   If she doesn't do anything, wait a few minutes and then try again.

3. **Clean up the potty immediately, but leave a little something behind.**

   You can leave a soiled newspaper or a scent cloth that you create by wiping your dog's bottom with a paper towel after she does the doo. Place this item just below the top layer of fresh newspaper or underneath the litter or grate. By doing so, you're telling your puppy where you want her to do her business. The smell of the soiled paper or litter is the canine equivalent of a come-hither glance.

4. **After your dog has pottied and you've cleaned the potty, let your puppy explore the house for a while.**

   But keep a close eye on her for signs that she needs to go again.

5. **If she suddenly displays signs that she needs to go, whisk her back to the potty and praise her if she pees or poops there. Give her a tiny treat, too.**

   The signs? Your dog stops, starts sniffing intently, begins to circle or pace, and/or starts to squat.

If you miss the signs that she's going to go and she has an accident, don't say anything. Just clean up and watch her more closely next time.

6. **After an hour or so of getting to know each other, put your puppy in her crate and let her take a much-needed nap.**

   Watch to see when she wakes up, though.

7. **When she wakes up, get her to her potty. If she uses it, praise and treat. Then clean up as before.**

Puppies need to potty after every meal, nap-time, and play session. Each time she uses her potty, praise her lavishly.

Scheduling bathroom breaks

Even indoor-trained dogs can benefit from learning to hold their poop and pee. The pooch with some self-control is much easier to live with than the dog with unregulated bathroom demands. Noticing that your dog may be ill is also easier if you can determine whether he's going more or less often than usual.

But regulating your dog's bathroom behavior doesn't have to flummox you. You can bring some order to your indoor trainee's life (and your own) by putting his trips to the potty on a schedule. Refer to the earlier section "Setting up a puppy potty schedule" and the section "Outdoor training for adult dogs" for your adult trainee.

Keeping your indoor potty area sanitary

Make sure that the puppy's potty spot remains sanitary. Here's how to keep it clean:

- ✔ Newspapers: Change the papers as soon as they're soiled (except for that pre-scented piece). If urine soaks through the papers to the shower curtain underneath it, just apply your pet stain cleaner to the dampened area and wipe it clean.

- ✔ Litter box: Plan on washing out the litter box with detergent and warm water at least once a week and on freshening the litter each time your dog uses the box.

- ✔ Grate/tray indoor potty: Rinse the grate and tray daily and wash them weekly unless the manufacturer's instructions dictate otherwise.

Avoiding Problems and Responding to Mistakes

Your puppy or dog undoubtedly is wonderful, but he isn't perfect. Inevitably, he'll deposit a puddle or pile away from the indoor potty. But take a deep breath. Repeat to yourself, "It's not his fault. It's not his fault." Take him to his crate and say nothing. Then go get some paper towels and pet-stain remover. Clean up according to the directions on the cleaner.

Above all, don't scold, punish, or try to correct your dog. He won't connect your loud voice and angry gestures with the fact that he went to the bathroom a mere ten minutes ago.

 If your dog folds back his ears and puts his tail between his legs while you let him know how upset you are, don't think — not for a minute — that he's feeling guilty. He's apprehensive, upset, maybe even fearful when you become angry, but he feels absolutely no remorse over doing what came naturally to him. So don't waste your breath — just clean up the mess.

Then ask yourself what you could've done to prevent your dog's accident. The following sections offer suggestions for some of the common mistakes humans make.

Ensure you provide adequate supervision

Until you know how well your dog can regulate her bathroom behavior, she needs your close supervision at all times, except when she's in her crate. Keep a close eye on her when she's not being confined. That way, you figure out what she's likely to do before she

deposits a puddle or pile, which can help you antici-
pate when she's about to do the doo.

 A good way to keep an eye on your dog as you
go from room to room is to attach a leash and
take her with you wherever you go in the
house.

Be consistent

Whether your house-training efforts are successful
depends almost solely on how you proceed. You can't
take a slapdash approach. If you're inconsistent, don't
give her the access she needs to the areas you want
her to go, or let her roam unsupervised all over your
house before she's ready for that freedom, you under-
mine your efforts. But by picking the right time to begin
house-training, knowing your dog's strengths and
weaknesses, and following the guidelines in the following section, you can put together a plan that's sure to
succeed.

Expand her concept of "home"

Fortunately for you, dogs don't like to soil their homes.
Unfortunately, dogs and humans have different defini-
tions of home. To you, your entire house is home —
even the rooms, like the guest bedroom or the formal
dining room, that you're rarely in.

Your dog doesn't use floor plans and plaster walls to
identify home; she uses her nose. Her home is where
the family smells are. If you spend lots of time in the
kitchen or the family room with her, she identifies that
place as a place she lives. Places where the family
smell is absent and — ding! ding! ding! We have a
winner! — any place that already smells like urine or
feces is a bathroom area to her.

So here's what you do to help your dog recognize the bathroom areas you approve of and to identify those areas that are off-limits:

✔ **Spend time in every room of your house with your dog.** Pick a room a night if you have to, and take in a book, sit on the floor, and keep your dog with you. The more she associates a room with you and the family, the less likely she'll be to think of it as an outhouse.

✔ **Identify the bathroom area you want her to use (inside or out) and take her there *every time* she has to go to the bathroom and treat her when she's done.** As she goes in the right spot, she leaves a bit of her scent — even if you clean it up. Pretty soon the smell, the repetition of going to the same place every time, and the reward she gets for doing well teach her where the best bathroom area is.

✔ **If she has an accident, clean up the mess and use an enzyme-based cleaning solution to eliminate the smell that will lure her back.** (Don't use ammonia, which smells like urine to a dog.) Then spend some time with your dog in that room to supplant any lingering bathroom smell with your smell.